ON
ONLY NIGHTS

ON
ONLY NIGHTS

Stories & Poems

Robert Cruess

ISBN-13: 978-1791616786

Printed in the United States of America

First Edition: 2018

Library of Congress Cataloguing in Publication Data:
A catalog record for this book is available from the
Library of Congress

to all those
who have had,
or will have
an "only night" —
i can guarantee
at least two   only nights,
the night you were born
and the night you will die.

but if you are clever   and
open   yourself to life...
i promise you hundreds
perhaps... thousands

of "only" nights.

"A Jug of Wine, a Loaf of Bread—and Thou"

— Omar Khayyám

Contents

on only nights

on a January night
long after midnight
   last cigarette in a gloved hand
   so cold i could feel
   a sting in my lungs
i saw the Milky Way's splendor
spill across the sky
above Chichester Hill.

it was an only night
   and though alone
   on the so dark hill
i could sense
   the presence of travelers all
   on our ovoid revolving
   through beauty beyond belief
   clinging to our starship Earth.

If you wanted to buy...

a small souvenir windmill and you were in San Antonio, I would suggest that you drive over to Blanco, find the restaurant with the old-fashioned porch overlooking the Green, pick out a good seat, and wait for the waitress.

A fortyish woman in a cotton print dress will come over and say, "Are you from around here, Honey? I don't think I've seen you before." And you can say, "And here I was trying to blend in, and you go and pick me out like a weevil in a cotton boll."

And the waitress will say, "My name is Amy Day, and I can tell that you would fit in here in Blanco—you have an easy way like us folks and in a few days, you'd be feeling like a native."

"Well thank you Amy Day," and you may say, "I do like the feel of Blanco, the people smile at me, the warm breezes soothe me, and the town almost feels like home. But before I order, I was wondering if you might know where I could buy a small souvenir windmill to remind me of this part of Texas?"

Amy Day will say, "You sure asked the right person, Honey, so give a listen—go North to Johnson City, turn left on Route 290, and continue on to the LBJ Ranch on the banks of the Pedernales River. You are gonna luv it. They have walking tours, cattle in the fields, and the best gift store around this part of Texas. I used to work there and one of the best sellers was a cute little windmill—you can put it on your porch and when those breezes come up, it will whirl and whirl and you will sit back and remember me and Blanco, Texas."

"Thank you, Amy Day," you will say. "I'll take that advice and, after lunch, I'll drive on up to the LBJ Ranch and buy that windmill I've been thinking about."

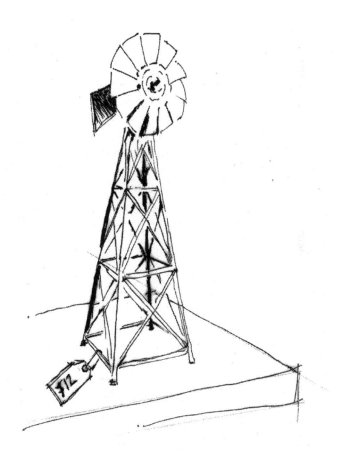

Lost... at sea

And there on the dance floor
Six stories above the sea
Marty and Marion,
M&M to their friends,
Have been in love
For over 60 years.
And she throws her arms
Around his neck
As his arms caress
Her spreading hips —
She lays her head
On boney shoulders worn by work,
And there on the dance floor,
They move as one
Upon a gentle sea.

No fear   not here
Dancing
On their sea of life,
But were there a fear
I know it would be
That one would be the first to die
And leave the other...
Lost at sea.

So seldom given

an unexpected   hand held
a flower sent
    with a scent to remember
a twice given smile with
    a kiss on the cheek.

let's go for a walk
    i'll listen as you talk
of plans for this   and
    plans for that
as our lives together
    unfold
the path.

the Traveler

how many times
have you asked me?
how often have i said
"i can't" —
but i've tried, and

one day in the trying
a voice said,
"i can tell that story,
i am the Traveler —
where you go   i go,
what you see   i see.
i know your truths   and untruths,
your deepest secrets,
hidden fears —
i can tell those stories."

so there you have it.
if i can't tell the story,
the Traveler can.

a rainbow ended

we arrived
on a day
when warmth
again embraced our lives
and a rainbow above
Half Moon Cay
ended its arc
on our spit of land
   and not upon the aqua sea.

Deal... or no deal

Well, the discussion wasn't really over, it was just late, and so, here I am again... the "Traveler," picking up the pieces of an unfinished story about the *energy* of the universe and "All-That-Is." So, I'll need your attention.

For the purpose of this discussion, there is no requirement for humans to be other than smart, or at least smart enough to understand and appreciate the *energy* that we, and the universe, and God all share. Sapiens all, we have evolved to that point where, collectively, we have a deep and fundamental understanding of energy. We are from the stars... we get it.

But what place does God have in our understanding? Is his/her *energy* of a type superior to ours? Let's assume that in this universe, God's *energy* is the same as ours, however, God has been around longer and, therefore, is more... knowing.

To get to the heart of the discussion, I'm going to use a thought experiment expounded by a friend of mine. Let's just call him, Robert. The title of his carefully crafted thought experiment is... "C'mon Man." Now, don't lose me just because the experiment's title doesn't appear to imply deep thought. Give me a chance to explain.

Here goes: God appears to Robert in the form of... Kenny Rogers, reprising his role as the *Gambler*—"Know when to hold 'em, know when to fold 'em, etc.," and Kenny

... I mean God, says, "Robert, I know that you are really interested in this God-eternity-infinity business and I know that you would like to know all that is, was, and will be. I can help you on your quest."

Robert says, "Really."

And God says, "I can see your skepticism, because you think there will be a price to pay, or as they say in the Old Testament, *Yahweh wants a sacrifice.* Well, you are correct because, in this particular universe, there is no such thing as a free lunch."

Robert says, "Fair is fair, and what might your Greatness want in return?"

"Robert, you know you are a part of me, just as I am a part of you, so you can dispense with the titles, however, here is the deal. I have decided to become the God of an alternate dimension, and I must replace MYSELF... oops, there I go with the ego thing again, but back to the point. I will require one of your children, and I will take him or her to the *guff*, which is the treasury of souls located in the seventh heaven. The child will know no pain, although every trace of their soul will disappear, and it is in this way that I will fall through the guff and reemerge in an alternate dimension where I will once again resume my role as GOD ... sorry, there I go again, I just had a power surge. But the point is, YOU will be God—you will have all my knowledge, all my power—is that cool or what?"

And Robert says, (don't tell me if you've guessed) he

says, "C'mon Man—are You Kiddin' me?"

God doesn't get many surprises, but Robert's response gave Him/Her something to think about.

Robert initially thought that he was something special because he had told God to take a hike rather than give up one of his children. Yes, it is impressive that a mere human would turn down an offer to be God. And he wondered, "Is it cooler to be human than to be God? So he tried his thought experiment on friends, associates, even a few academics. He was surprised to find that most would not take the deal.

It is staggering to comprehend that most people would turn down the deal to be God, rather than cash in one of their children. So as I see it, the result of the thought experiment means either; (a) being God isn't that big a deal, (b) we are already God and we don't need to take the deal, or (c) in our hearts we know... there is no God.

Give it a try—God, in the form of Kenny Rogers, decked out with spurs and a fancy cowboy hat, ambles into your living room and offers you the deal. What do you say?

Deal, or no deal?

Talk to ya down the line,

The Traveler

You gotta take her

"Somewhere where /
She's never been before"
From "Words of Love," sung by Mama Cass...
Well then,
How 'bout Arkansas?
We'll cross the cicatrice of America
    Memphis to Arkansas —
Like starlings
From above we'll see it all —
The ever moving great and muddy
Mighty Mississippi.
Now close your eyes—feel the power beneath
    Open your eyes and
There is Arkansas—flat fertile... all arable land and...
Playground of Bill and Hill —
Squint your eyes and there they are   driving
Incognito in a '74 Ford pickup along I-40 —
Goin' up to Memphis—girl's gonna go shoppin'
At Lansky's—go walkin'
Down Beale Street—bar-hoppin' at B.B. King's, then
Out to Graceland... Doesn't everyone?
Isn't everyone looking... for Elvis?

Isn't everyone looking for...

Postcards

Here comes the sun
   Drawing sweat from my pores
Cancering my skin
   Warming my bones
Turning my mind
   Toward life

Key Largo   we're here
   & it's on the radio
& we sing along —
 a bit off tune —
not giving a damn   we
   as free as herons
   high overhead —
   walking   on white sand
   smelling   the blue of the ocean
& we "have it all
   like Bogey and Bacall."

Have you heard
   My thoughts   my voice
     Across the thousand miles?
 I think it can be done —
   My touch   my breath
 I've posted on the wind.

If I could remember
   What lonely is
   Or lonely was
I know
   I'd love you more...
   Than I do

I'll hold you
      And you'll hold me
      Through nights of love
      And sacred dreams.

In the mid-world
   Between dreams
   And dreams of dreams
I have your softness
   Thoughts of love —
   Real or perceived
And your unmanliness
I hold
   In the mirror
   Of the dream
Where I return home
   To your soul searching bed
And you paint my body
   ...With a womanly scent.

flutter

ibus in the front yard
crane
one-legged in the pond
geckoes abound
alligator   not yet found
clouds rising high
in an afternoon sky
and the lazy days
like butterflies...

flutter me by.

Me and Roseanne

Sittin' on the porch
Sun going down   all alone
With the music of Roseanne Cash
   (I enjoy listening— she can't talk back)
Just me and the trees,
And a hummingbird hungry
   For a sunset snack.

If Roseanne
Could hear me
I'd talk   of Southern nights
Cafe lights   in Oxford
Cotton dresses shaped by warm breezes,
A mint julep in a steady hand,
And she might
Mention   Tupelo, or Jackson —
I'd bring up Hattiesburg…
   Maybe Choctaw Ridge —
See if she knew
Why Billy Joe
Did what he did?
We might joke about
The last time I saw Elvis
And wasn't that him
   On the Tallahatchie Bridge?

"Can I get you another Mint Julep?
The night, dear lady
   Is oh so young."

Texas Hill Country

is a place   for babies and dogs
for Sturgill Simpson singin'
    "thank you, God
    for my life of sin."
where brown-eyed Texas Longhorns
    study   my aura
    pose for the camera   in my hand.

where cowboys ride Rams, and
Silverados
gather, beer in hand
down at the grain tower,
or along the arroyo
at ease in the shade
of sycamores, cottonwoods
and spindly cedars.

at the Old 300
in Blanco   the brisket
is better than brisket should be
and cowboys and girls
in wide-brimmed hats
pull up in trucks   (we don't call 911)
walk Texas style to a table —
order up a Sunday meal
    hold hands and say grace
    before the bread is broken.

No pretend cowboys   'round here.

Nights like these

Jays huddled in a hemlock
Sparrow under eaves —
Oh they must desire life
To live
Through nights like these.

Music in the wind

On the ridge of the
Hill maybe   an arête
    The Masters of all
    (in our own minds at least)
We survey   a world
That appears to be
Ours   but then
Come the winds from the valley rising
Pushing black clouds backlit eerie orange
From
Over the Monadnocks ascending
    Lightning jumping from the sky
    To the highest landforms... ah...
That would be us.

And then to wonder
Why
We chose the house
Atop the hill?

It was because   of the music
    The music in the wind.

California Postcards

so high —
i don't know why
above galaxies of towns
in an endless universe.

Malibu morning —
wrecked on a beach
here by the Sea
at the edge of the Earth.

all hawks in a blue
sky above fire burnt   earth
black bush huddling
by a turned and twisted Joshua tree
all life in a struggle —
as life must be.

weathered
old man that i am —
just an old desert being
on the beach of a poisoned sea.

sunflowers, cotton
pumpkins by the sea
an only one daughter
for my soul's company —
    we have no why
    no when no where
why us dear god?   nor care.

i'm only a man
    standing
in dead man's shoes —
    shoes
i've worn since birth.

down on the boulevard
huddling
in the street   fear —
waiting
for the nightfall.

is the rainbow there
    for the flowers to see?
why is grass   grass?
or trees   trees?
    all of everything
    seems to me
ever too perfect —
than there is a need
    to be.

Earthquake

As windows shake
Lamps fall and all
The room moves
   Like a rag doll
   In a big dog's mouth
People
   Like ants move
   Through shards
   Of glass broken
   From buildings   beyond
Their existence   and control,
   (like ants we have none)
Cry and or scream
   In a state beyond fear
We hold
each other
   In the marginal light
   Of a flickering candle

AND WAIT

   and wait

and the twisted steel
   & bodies beneath
   concrete collapsed -
seems worlds   away.

From Death Valley

how totally alone
   in the expanse of space
we are

even the billions
of stars
in our galaxy floating   rotating
toward Andromeda
are no more than a handful
of sand
on an endless beach

and from Death Valley
one can see   can feel
the depth
the proof of aloneness
in the breathtaking magic

of a true Dark Sky.

Myron and his mule

wandering   waterless
Sister Jenny in tow
Myron to himself   mutters,
    "where is the mother lode?
    my fortune
    would be
    a canteen of water   cool and clear
    water."

"but, i fear,   Sister Jenny...
we are lost —
and brine won't slake
my thirst
nor yours."

aloud he says,
to blistering sands and Sister Jenny,
"will our remains
be found?"

"of course not good Sista' —
we know the desert
we know the Valley of Death...
and the just rewards of those
who fail...

the desert will leave no trace."

i'd people the stars

imagine an after-death
with all of light⠀⠀all of knowledge, and
 all the power that can possibly be —
well, there would be alright
⠀⠀nothing
⠀⠀to learn
⠀⠀no adventure⠀⠀nowhere to grow
⠀⠀you already know⠀⠀it all.

so first
i would create
man and then man's mate.
oh, i'd people
⠀⠀the stars
⠀⠀with questioning souls,
bid them surmise

my nature and my goals.

And if she has said... "No."

Luis Umberto was an acquaintance of mine, during the time I worked in Venezuela. He was a Landscape Architect, and although he didn't appear very smart... he was. He told me that he had been a chess champion in Puerto Rico. When we both had business in Caracas, we would go out at night to cafés on Sabana Grande and smoke cigars, drink rum, talk politics, and play chess until well after midnight. Those were my kind of nights.

One time when we were in Caracas on the weekend, he suggested that we go to Parque del Este to see one of the recent works of the famous Landscape Architect, Roberto Burle Marx. So, on a pleasant Saturday afternoon, we were off to the Park. The work of Burle Marx was amazing at that time. He had designed a large ceramic wall with water spouts coming out of it, and adjacent gardens replete with multicolored flowers and tropical plants. It was the first time that Luis had seen Burle Marx's work in person, and he was in awe. And although I was not in awe, I was very impressed. This visit to Parque del Este happened in 1969.

Forty-seven years later, I'm with my wife in New York City, and being a Landscape Architect, she suggested that we go to the Jewish Museum on 5th and 92nd to see an exhibit of the work of Roberto Burle Marx. The exhibit included many of his drawings and sketches for his park designs, as well as some of his jewelry and tapestry creations.

In a corner of one of the exhibit rooms, there was a large book of his works, and the book was opened to the pages that showed his work at... Parque del Este. Amazing! What are the chances of that happening? In 1969, I never could have imagined that 47 years later I would be at a museum in NYC that was displaying his work on the Venezuelan Park. That kind of coincidence gets me thinking about "The Path Not Taken," by Robert Frost, or the multiverse theories related to quantum mechanics. Those theories posit that every time a serious choice is made, the alternate choice continues in a parallel world. In other words, had I not chosen to go to Parque del Este, there would have been another me that continued along a life-line where I had opted not to visit the Park. If you follow this kind of speculative reasoning, there are millions of me(s) and you(s) inhabiting the multiverse.

Later that same day, my wife and I were ambling around NYC through the noonday heat, and we stumbled upon The Boat Basin in Central Park. It is a pleasant place for lunch with distant views to the Bethesda Terrace. There is the added benefit of watching tourists try to maneuver around in their rented rowboats, like bumper cars on water.

There was a couple in a rowboat drifting near the restaurant patio, and the man stood up in the boat and then proceeded to kneel—clearly he was proposing. The surrounding crowd got caught up in what was happening—and when the woman in the boat threw her arms around the man, clearly accepting the proposal—the crowd cheered, they clapped, some women started to cry and or, yell, some kissed their boyfriend or husband—the couple on the boat waved to all the witnesses on the shore.

I was spending more time watching the crowd than watching the couple, and I was thinking about the huge granite outcropping on the opposite shore. Most people don't know that if you examine the outcropping on the far side of the basin, you can see the glacial tracks from the last glaciation which occurred some 15,000 years ago, and to me, that made this place heavy with time, and time gives a "power" to the Boat Basin.

If one were to select a place to propose, this would be an excellent choice. So my feeling was, the couple had made a good decision to start their new lives in this location, and if I was right, they should have a long and successful marriage.

And then lunch came, and I focused on the couple floating across the pond, setting out on a new life-line, but I couldn't escape the thought that an "alternate" life-line existed, where the woman had said... "No."

The Bridge

It was Sunday, July 20th, 1969. I was sitting on a Naugahyde sofa in a very poor Barrio in Cumana, Venezuela, watching an old black and white TV, with a smallish joint as my only companion. As I suspect you may know, I was watching the moon landing—none of the people in the Barrio cared, because they all knew that... it was really taking place in Arizona. "Digame Roberto, tu sabes que la luna queda en Arizona."

After all the news about the moon landing, there was a hint of some problem in the USA having to do with a car accident involving Teddy Kennedy. Evidently, on the night of July 18th,1969, while the US astronauts were en route to the moon, Kennedy had a serious accident, but details were lacking... at least in the Venezuelan press.

A decade later, I'm flying home from a trip to Spain. I went by myself and wandered around the country for a couple of weeks. I practiced my Spanish, enjoyed the beauty of the Country, and embraced my hours of solitude.

The return flight was on a Boeing 747 Jumbo Jet, a remarkable aircraft. I completely enjoyed the flight, and as we began our descent into JFK International Airport, the pilot said, "If you look off to your left, you have a good view of the famous Chappaquiddick Bridge." I was on the left side of the plane in a window seat, and sure enough, there was the bridge—the bridge that may have altered the history of the United States, because now, Teddy Kennedy... would never be President. And that may be good, or it may be bad, but without a doubt, history was changed.

In spite of the Chappaquiddick... incident, Kennedy did decide to run for President in 1980, and of course, that meant coming to New Hampshire. At that time, I was the Assistant Chief Engineer of the Environmental Agency, and our Department was one among several located in the Health and Welfare Building in Concord, NH. On a Thursday afternoon, around 2 PM, Teddy and his entourage showed up at the building to do a meet-and-greet with some of the State employees.

My boss, for whatever reason, did not want to take the time to usher Kennedy around the building, so I became the designated greeter. I went out to the lobby and introduced myself to Senator Kennedy. He was pleasant and all that, and he asked me if I could take him around to meet some of the employees.

There was a large cafeteria in the building where employees would take extended coffee breaks and, in many instances, hold informal meetings with the public. As we moved through the cafeteria, Kennedy was beaming—he was a fish back in the water—he exuded charisma, he was the flesh and blood definition of charisma, tall, handsome, powerful, completely in control... the last vestige of a legend, and... he knew it.

But New Hampshire people are a tough audience.

They have seen charisma before, they have endured long and difficult winters—they know that there are consequences for serious missteps in life. They were all polite to the Senator, they noted his importance, but they were not dumbstruck by the Kennedy legend. I was surprised because I was reveling in the significance of escorting a legend—the last son—the brother of Jack and Bobby, both of whom I had supported.

After about an hour of introductions, and a lot of small-talk, I began to view him the way most of the other workers did... he was flawed. He was dragging a bridge around behind him, even when smiling or shaking hands... the shadow of the Bridge was there. I knew, at that moment, he would never be President.

Now, some four decades later, I'm watching the movie "Chappaquiddick," and it all rings true. Bruce Dern, portraying the father, Joseph P. Kennedy, is listening to Teddy's explanation about the incident at Chappaquiddick. Teddy desperately wants his father's love and understanding—he leans over and kisses his father on the forehead, and the father, now a stroke victim, whispers in his ear... "You will never be a great man."

The 1980 Democratic Primary in NH did not go Teddy's way, even though he was from the adjoining State of Massachusetts. Around the country, Jimmy Carter gave Teddy a whuppin'—Carter won 36 primaries, while only 12 were won by Kennedy.

Teddy never ran for President again.

"so," she says,

"i need your help."

and obviously,
what can i say
but, "yes—one half hour
no more no less
to plant
a daffodil cloud."

and as the sweat
rolled off my brow,
as hours passed,
no gain to curse
a promised yellow cloud,

just bite my lip,
wait for Spring,
and the emerging beauty

of a daffodil cloud.

Easter

midday   & heat
swallows me whole
& all the beach bathing
barely clad
women in the world
can't distract

my afternoon peace,

and life of ease
    in another time —
zone   without marching
    my life to the factory —
my bed
    bed sweating wet
    in the light of
    a tropical
moon sucking breezes
through coconut palms

—just waiting for Easter.

white moon
& a white cross
hanging
    over Little Havana
& baby   screaming
full car careening
joyeria!   muebleria!

Christ —   we only need milk!

Good Friday   Holy
Saturday   who said,
"it's easy to be a mother?"
    (i don't think it was Mary!)

but we are coming home -
for Easter.
    & a new and different   life
Together.

Divination... twice!

Saint Teresa of Avila was considered one of the mystics of the Catholic Church in the 1500s. She wrote of her devotions which enabled her to be as one with God.

The devotions consisted of 1.) the devotion of the heart, essentially mental prayer, 2.) the devotion of peace, essentially being of service to God, 3.) the devotion to union, which is to be absorbed in God, and 4.) the devotion of ecstasy, which involves leaving the physical body behind and living in the spiritual world.

"Well, isn't that interesting?" one might say, facetiously. I would say, "It is interesting, because she was dealing with mystical events, and few people give much credit to mysticism or, for that matter, any event that can't be explained by science."

In the mid-1500s, Saint Teresa was offered a tract of land upon which to build a new convent. However, there was no water on the property, and that was of much concern to Teresa. She was pondering the problem when a Friar Antonio approached her because he had heard of her dilemma. He went up to Teresa carrying a three-pronged, Y-shaped branch in his hand. He told her that with the branch he held in his hand, he could find water on the property, i.e. through *Divination. It should be noted that there were those who said divination might be explained by the intervention of Satan.*

34

However, divination is not that far from mysticism, and so Teresa let him have a go at it and sure enough, Antonio and his divining rod—the 3-pronged, Y-shaped branch—soon located a potential source of water. Antonio told them to dig in that location, and... there it was, a gusher of water that could sustain a convent.

Antonio's prowess with the 3-pronged branch may, or may not, have been the beginning of dowsing, or modern divination, or... quackery.

I would expect that almost everyone has heard of dowsing, and I further suspect that most people view it as... a scam. And that brings us to the point of the story, namely *Dowsing*.

It was 1972, and I had purchased a house in Dunbarton, NH—a fixer-upper with spectacular views of the White Mountains. And on a clear day, I could see the coal-black smoke from the cog railway as it ascended Mount Washington. What a deal, however, there was a catch. The house got its water from the farmhouse across the street and, as part of the deal to buy the house, I had to drill my own well, properly disconnect, and then cap the existing waterline connection.

I hired a well driller—an old-timer name of Leland who had drilled many wells in Dunbarton. I told him about the problem we faced, which was to find and properly disconnect the water line from the main farmhouse across the street, and we had to do that without knowing where the pipe was located. It obviously crossed under the street, crossed the front lawn of the house I was buying, and then passed through the foundation, under the concrete floor, and emerged at the far side of the cellar. It was impossible to tell where the pipe entered the house.

I was thinking, "What a dilemma. We can't drive the huge drill rig over the lawn, because it would crush the existing water supply that I wanted to keep using until the new well was drilled, tested and connected to a new pressure tank in the cellar."

"Well, Leland," I said, "What are we going to do?"

"No problem," he said, and he walked over to a black walnut tree. "One of my favorites," he said and proceeded to break off a 3-pronged, Y-shaped branch. He examined the branch and appeared quite satisfied with his acquisition.

"So," I said, "What are you going to do with the branch?"

He said, "Since it is your property, you are going to find the underground pipe," and he handed me the branch.

"Really?" I said.

Leland looked me in the eye and said, "You look like a dowser to me."

Leland instructed me on how to hold the dowsing rod, and then told me to walk across the front yard, arms extended, and with the intent to find the underground waterline. Off I went, arms in front of me, maybe three feet apart, and I was feeling... stupid.

And then... the branch started twitching in my hands, completely out of my control—I was astounded, bewildered, confused—the piece of wood was literally trying to jump out of my hands. I was struggling to control it, who, or whatever was in charge here. The front prong of the branch was pointing straight down and the black walnut dowsing stick was pulling me toward the ground.

I freaked out and simply dropped the branch.

"Nice going," Leland said, "The pipe will be right below this spot," and he makes a mark. "Are you sure?" I asked. Leland said, "Watch this," and he went to the opposite side of the front yard, with the dowsing rod, maybe forty feet away, and he walked toward me. As he got near the spot where the rod had almost jumped out of my hands, the branch in Leland's hands began twitching again, and even Leland was having a hard time controlling it. "Like I told ya," he said, "black walnut makes for the best dowsing rod there is."

Okay, I'm an engineer with a Masters in Civil Engineering. I've studied physics, calculus, dynamics, etc., and I'm scientifically oriented, therefore, what just happened was... inexplicable. The dowsing rod was clearly in charge—I was a vehicle. Leland said, "Yeah, it is a little spooky the first time you do it, but I done it hundreds-a-times. Now, I can even spot dowsers, when I see them, and

Robert, you my friend... are a dowser."

Later that day, he brought in a small backhoe and dug very slowly, so as not to break the waterline. After only a few minutes, he was scraping the pipe. Wow! To me, this was more than magic. It wasn't just a trick, it was actual... *divination.*

The next day, the drill rig was brought in, and we didn't have to cross the pipe. He picked a good spot, set up the rig and started drilling. A few hundred feet down, we hit water. A few days later, the pipes to the new well were installed. We capped the old pipe, and my contract was satisfied.

But, I was left perplexed. There was no physical way that I could conceive that a black walnut branch could possibly have known, or could have possibly been attracted to, the location of the underground waterline. I resolved never to dowse again. I didn't like the feeling of having been under the complete control... of a black walnut, three-pronged, Y-shaped branch.

As time passed, I would occasionally think of that dowsing experience in Dunbarton, but it was always an uncomfortable subject to think about, and I would quickly banish the thought.

Thirty-four years later, I was working on a development in Bedford, NH, and it required a well. I hired a well driller and met him at the property in order to explain the constraints, namely, setbacks from property lines, and setbacks from the proposed septic system. Danny, the driller said, "With all these constraints, I better dowse the property so that I get it right." Okay, now I'm getting goosebumps, and creepy thoughts, as I'm confronted with another non-scientific situation. I thought dowsing was dead.

Danny goes over to the edge of the property, surveys the trees, walks back and forth very deliberately. Finally, he stops at an old, gnarly, cherry tree. He breaks off a... three-pronged, Y-shaped branch and... it's deja-vu all over again. He fondles the branch, toys with it in his hands until it feels comfortable, and then he walks towards me.

"Ever dowsed before?" he asked. I kind of stuttered, and said, "Well, uh, sort of," and he said, "I thought so," and he handed me the specially configured... cherry branch.

Reluctantly, I took the branch, and I told him it was over 30 years ago since I last dowsed. "Don't matter," he said, "you either can or you can't, but I'm betting you can, cuz you look like a dowser to me."

"I'm a civil engineer," I said. Then feeling really stupid, and knowing I am about to embarrass myself, I took the cherry branch and headed toward the general area where we could drill a well and still meet all the setback requirements. I was just being casual, and I wanted to get the embarrassment over with, and then, and then... it can't be—it simply can't be, but, the twitching began, and the branch was taking control of the situation. It wanted to jump out of my hand.

Danny came alongside me and said, "Looks like you've found a good vein."

"You think so?" I said. "Do you want to verify that?"

"No need," said Danny, "I saw it for myself," and he dropped his tool belt in the very spot where the dowsing rod now quietly rested. I reached down, picked up the branch, and gave it to Danny, and he said, "Nice job Mr. Engineer... or should I say, Mr. Dowser?"

By the following afternoon, we had an eight gallon per minute well, which is a lot of water to find in an area where the average well produced less than ½ gallon per minute. I had evidently detected, or rather my three-pronged, Y-shaped, cherry stick had detected a mother lode vein of water.

"Impossible," you say, and I would agree, and yet... and yet—it did happen—and not just once, but twice.

Of God... or not

As interesting and compelling
As foxes can be,
I'm a thankful Sapien.
I know the distances to
And movements of
Planets and stars.
I ponder
The origin of all that is —
The beginning of time,
Its ultimate end
I conceive   of God... or not.

And the fox imagines
The fullness...
Of his or her
Next meal.

The Shuttle Explosion

January 28, 1986
    the newspaper

two teens in Town
    down at the Trailways
    and hanging around
on Tuesday night
    in Christa's Town.
the Indian head
    is under the Dome
    flashing the time
for all the drifters
    who still can see,
while the bum-under-the-ramp
    curls up in his bag
smokes a last cigarette
    then crumples the news
stuffs it under his head.

    And who…
Who would believe the news that said,
    "Christa…
Christa is dead."

The Shuttle Explosion

January 28, 1986
   the TV

it talks of death
like a neighbor used to do
   it speaks...
   and we cry
for heroes never met
although we have seen them laugh
and laughing stroll
through the family room.
now we see them   explode
   Again   and Again and Again
until we no longer know...

were they really   real?

washed by the light

through the field fog
of near dawning
    her imagined breath
    upon an unkempt face

he is alone   going home
bathed in love
washed by the light
from a slip of a moon
dying from the dawning

    of another day entering.

Coach

And here we are...
29 years since Anne said,
   "I'm in labor... it's time."

We went to the hospital, I guess
   Around midnight.
Anne went to prep, and I
Did what all
   Helpless fathers do...
In a daze I found
The coffee machine.

I took the coffee to the waiting
   Room and there were others —
Clueless males on time-worn sofas
Thumbing Ladies Home Journal and People
Magazines
Stale coffee still
In hand   eyes glassy.

A nurse walks in, says, "Robert,
   Or should I say, Coach?"
"Coach," I say... "It gives me purpose."

Four hours later —
I'm sweating   getting
Ice   "breathe in   breathe out... pant."
"Fuck you," she says
("You can't talk to the Coach like that,"

I mumble.)

She said it again,
And then —
There's blood   I faint.

Some minutes later,
    Recovered I guess,
They hand the Coach   a barrel-chested
Squirming squealing brand new   boy.

having died

few are those
who recall the breaking of the water
and the tumult and trauma
of birth,
but i do —
although i speak from beyond
where all is known
from long before i was.

having died young,
here meaning 65,
my family and friends
gathered to recall,
with stories   that when told,
drew laughter
that lessened the tears,
of those
that pined for me.

and in truth,
if truth hereafter be,
i watched the service
without emotion —
no joy   no loss
i simply am
and will always be
Trapped
...in eternity.

i'll be sitting at dinner...

or at an immensely
important meeting
and i'll respond to an inane   question, and
realize   Christ   i sound like
my father, or
i turn   and see my reflection —
my eyes
in a cracked bar mirror
staring back   at me,
judging me   through the very eyes
of my soul.
but i've seen that soul before —
it's my father's not mine...

am i the soul of my father?   was he
the soul of his father and maybe the same
soul...
all the way down.

Aromatherapy

There was Ken and
Davey, his girl Trudy
The lawyer Sabrina
And the bit players
Mounsey and Nick.
All of them rich—at least
Richer than me   no need
For my money boys
And girls —
Not enough to change
Your life
Like a brand new wife or
A dirk through the sternum —
The smell of money...
Was their reward.

The barbarian's heart

around a corner, behind a door or
so close i can smell it   taste it   embrace
it—but i don't—which is not to say i've
not tried it   succumbed to the siren's
call   of quick riches   or vigilante
justice   meted out to the
deserving.
but, it doesn't work for me—there are
times i want to take my foot and shove
it so far up someone's ass... that,
well, i don't even have the words   but
i don't do it.
if i even think about it too much...
something bad... happens to me!
i am not the one to be with
when Attila, or his ilk, is out and about.
but, i acknowledge the aggression
of those who can confront the barbarian —
i acknowledge those
who can eat an adversary's evil heart... "belch"

and go on with life.

Las Vegas

Most often when I visited Las Vegas it would be on business and, generally, my business would be related to meeting with retail developers.

It was several years ago that I was in Las Vegas meeting with four developers who were based out of Miami, but were exploring new retail development opportunities in NH. They were looking for an engineering firm to do all their permitting work, and that is the type of work I do. I viewed the meeting as a good opportunity to secure work for my company.

I met with them on and off for a couple of days, and on their last night in Vegas they asked if I would be the designated driver while they did a night on the town. I quickly agreed to their request, in part to further the business relationship, and also because I had no need to experience the after-effects of a long party night.

The owner of the development company wasn't going to participate, so I would be driving his minions. The associates were... Jonathan, a very straight guy who happened to be a Quaker and had never been to a strip club; Bernie, a middle-aged, Jewish guy from Miami who had spent more time in strip clubs than at synagogue—he had Kenny G type, long dark hair and was a self-acknowledged expert on... everything; and lastly, there was Danny, a fortyish guy from Ohio who had just done a major Home Depot deal, so he was feeling like a big-time developer.

Around 10 PM on their last night in Vegas, they decided that it was time to go out on the Town. I grabbed the keys to the big white Cadillac with red leather interior. I felt a bit like a pimp, but I reoriented my thinking and assured myself that I was a "professional chauffeur."

Stop #1—"Crazy Horse"—a strip club. I dropped them off in front and was directed to a parking spot where I could wait for them. I told the guy that I would be there for a couple of hours.

The attendant said, "Look, man, can you do me a favor? I want to run out and see my girlfriend. It will take about half an hour, so would you be the attendant? Nothing to it—put the limos over on the left and direct the private cars to the lot on the right. Some people will give you a tip if you let them park nearer to the club in the VIP lot. You can keep whatever you get."

"Sounds OK to me," I said, "But keep it to less than an hour, I can't keep my guys waiting."

So, there I was, directing limos to the lot on the left, and cars to the lot on the right.

A limo guy pulls up next to me and says, "Hey man, any chance to park close so I can see my guys when they come out?"

"Well, ah... you know... ah," I said, and out comes a twenty dollar bill!

"I can make an exception," I said. "Park over there in the VIP lot."

And so it went for the next hour and a half until the real attendant returned, by which time I had pocketed $200 worth of "tips." I was thinking, "I'm good at this. I could make $600 a night if I put my mind to it."

My guys emerge around 1 AM and I was ready to drive them home, but... not happening. They are well oiled and want to visit another club. They are my potential clients, so... off we go to the Palomino Club.

After two or so hours at the Palomino, the tipsy trio shuffle out to the parking lot. Bernie insists that I give him the keys to the Caddy. He had rented the car and wanted the pleasure of driving it one more time before returning it in the morning. Reluctantly, I relinquished the keys—Wrong.

Bernie says, "I'm shows yous what this carrr can do!" He hits the gas and off we go down Paradise Boulevard—I see the speedometer hit 80 MPH, then blue lights from an oncoming car flash on. The cop is so pissed he jumps the median.

Bernie says, "Not to worrys, I gots it coveraged." Bernie pulls over—cop pulls over—Bernie jumps out of the car—WRONG.

The cop goes nuts—"Down on the ground, NOW." His hand is on his gun.

Bernie is saying, "but, but... " The cop says, "Shut up, lie still, or you get cuffed."

The other officer comes over to the passenger side of the Caddy.

I say, "Officer, can I say something?"

He says, "Sure, but it better be good."

I said, "I'm the designated driver, I haven't had a drink in 24 hours. The problem is... I ate something and then threw up on the Palomino parking lot. The guy on the ground grabbed the keys from me because I puked. As you can see, I'm fine now and very capable of driving to the hotel."

The officer says, "Are you suggesting we should let him go?"

I replied, "If there is any way to just give him a warning, that would be great. I can get us back to the Luxor. If not, then so be it.

The cop leaves to talk to the other cop. Bernie is off the ground, but is bent over the trunk.

After a few minutes, officer No.1 returns and asks me to get out of the car. He checks me out, asks a few questions, then hands me the keys. "Get these guys back to the hotel... NOW."

"Thank you," I said, as I stuffed Bernie into the front passenger seat. I then drove away... slowly, very slowly.

Epilogue

They hired my firm.

Leaving Las Vegas

After the Bernie ordeal (see the previous story), I had breakfast at the hotel, showered, changed, and headed to the Convention Center for the first of several meetings.

I had now been awake for more than 24 hours straight.

I slugged around the Convention Center until after noontime, and at lunch, I found a table in the corner of the cafeteria, laid my head on the table, and nodded off for a few treasured minutes. After the brief nap, I went back on the floor until 4 PM, and then grabbed a cab to the airport to catch a red-eye flight to Atlanta. In Atlanta, the plan was to change planes and fly to New York City for a meeting on some environmental topic at the Marriott Marquis.

By the time I got on the plane, I was hallucinating from sleep deprivation. I found my way to the last row of seats and collapsed in an aisle seat on the port side of the plane.

Before falling asleep, I remember thinking, "I've never had a feeling of nostalgia when leaving Las Vegas—it always seems like the right thing to do." And then I fell... into a coma-like sleep.

Sometime during the night, one of the passengers got up and went to the luggage storage above my seat. When he opened the bin, a heavy, tan briefcase with bronze corner caps fell out. The briefcase landed on my forehead just above my right eye—the impact woke me from my deep sleep. I could feel the warm blood running down my face—there was blood on my shirt.

The perpetrator looked at me and sensed that I was, perhaps, out-of-control... pissed.

I picked up the briefcase and walked towards him. By now, I must have looked as if I had survived an attempted ax murder.

He says as he retreats, "Is there anything I can do?"

I replied, "Yes there is. I would like to take this briefcase and give you a whack in your fuckin' head."

By then the crew reacted and escorted me back to my seat. They began to attend to the gash on my forehead. They wiped the blood and put a butterfly bandage on the wound. They asked me to fill out a report. I said, "Here's the deal—leave me alone, I'll be fine—don't ask me if I'm OK, don't call a doctor in Atlanta, simply... leave... me... alone. If you take the deal, you will never hear from me again. If you don't take the deal, my lawyers will be talking to the airline in the morning."

They took the deal.

Me and the bear

And the bear
Oblivious
To my presence
Crosses the field
While I mow the tall grass —
They just don't care anymore —
The whole country
Is their Yellowstone Park.
Now come the turkeys,
The crows   don't care.
A fox stands still
By the edge of the woods eyeing
    The deer and her fawn
As they graze in the orchard
    They don't care.
I feel like a bear
    An animal
Among animals.

Perhaps...
All is
As It should be.

water as far

as i can see
and the breadth
and immensity of the waters —
where   do you know
did the waters come from?

Comets,
comets they say, and
had there been
more comets
they say,
there would be no land
to greet the sea.

only the waves
and only clouds   in the sky
passing by.

oh what a loss
that would be —
no beaches to be walked
no hands of lovers held
no little dreams to be shared
no fields to run
or days... in the sun,

only the waves
and only the clouds
... passing by.

Perdido [Lost]

like back
streets of Oslo
or Tangiers at mid-
night   Arabs out
of their minds   deals
going down... demeaning
little deals
for a handful of Dirhams
or dollars for just
a few...
minutes of diversion.

Perdido by Ellington
on my Walkman
in some seedy park
       by the sea.

living the dream

bodies basking
in the warmth from our star
living and breathing   our life
   that came from the sea.

my daughter dreaming
   a dream of boys —
my son riding
   in white waves
   till his lips turn blue as the sky
   and my wife and i
   ponder
the why and the who
that we are.

overhead
the sun
like a vulture
circles my head —
seagulls
cast shadows
darting and darkening the sands —
and the soft flesh of women
bared   for my sun shaded eyes.

our baby sleeps
through torrential rains
and the ever dampness of naught-to-do
tuesday afternoon   but watch

clouds swirl and morph.

    — i could...
    think about money —
    payroll next Thursday,

or lie
mindlessly
alive but not.

fuck it   i'm ready —
    for a double-wide
    in a low-class park —
plastic   flamingos   wooden   bent-over-ladies
reflected
in the ball-on-a-pedestal   beer
in my hand in the hammock
    the widow
    making my lunch   living and dying
    from cigarette smoke and all night sex.

    OR

i could look out to sea
and into the moon...
that follows me home

and do what must be done.

Vasco da Gama

I can see   the São Gabriel
Sailing down   Rio Tejo
At the bow of the ship   the Admiral
Vasco da Gama   his sword hangs
By his side, beard trimmed,
Tricorn hat adjusted just so   he
Looks into a setting sun that colors
The open sea
White, yellow and gold,
But it is the white   monstrous fogbank
A mile offshore   that unnerves
The crew, and
The Captain says, "Don't worry boys —
It's only fog, no giants be there.
Turn to port as we near the fog,
India is our goal   treasure is our task."

Sail on   Sail on
          And they did.

A soft breath

Of orange light
Touches the red-brown
Plains of España
Caressing   then waking
The now yellow-green   soon
To be purple   olives
Warming
In the rising of Ra
And in the west
A still full moon surveys
The bounty of Spain.

And my shadow falls
Upon the reddish earth
The very earth
Where Columbus, Magellan
Elcano   and all
The New World Explorers
Walked.

Bravo España
Bravo Seville!

Red Earth

The cities of the sea
Left Miami and pointed south
To Cozumel, Costa Maya,
Puerto Rico and all the
So warm islands.

Our ship turned north
And east
Like Columbus
Returning to Spain —
Though we have no treasures
Other than memories worn by time.

And we drift through the Triangle —
"Where there be powers
To lure a ship
Into the abyss,"

But for now
All is peaceful
Just a gentle roll   an easy pitch
And like Columbus   we long
For the red earth
Of Spain.

*Graffiti**

Si vienes buscando batalla
   If you are looking for a fight
Yo soy la batalla
   I am the fight
Si vienes buscando amor
   If you are looking for love
Yo soy el amor
   I am all love
No camino con nadie porque
   I go through life alone because
Tengo mi propio camino
   I have my own path
Tengo de negro
   The black are a part of me
Tengo de blanco
   The white are a part of me
Tengo de chino
   The chinese are a part of me
No tengo nada
   I have nothing
Porque nada soy
   Because I am nothing
No camino con nadie
   I walk alone
Tengo mi propio camino
   I have my own path
Y ya tengo mi amigo
   And I have my friend

Que sabe
Do you understand

Que nada soy
I am nothing

*My translation of graffiti on a wall at a Santaria gathering on the outskirts of Havana, Cuba.

Diego

He guessed that I was an American, and so he came up to me and asked if I would change a few US dollars for some Cuban Convertible Currency, CUCs and pronounced kooks. I was amazed at how good his English was, after all, he was just a Havana street sweeper.

I agreed to take his US dollars and give him an equal number of CUCs, but being curious I asked where he had learned his English, and he said, "In Milwaukee." It is difficult for Cubans to leave Cuba, so I asked him how he happened to get to Milwaukee. Diego asked me if I remembered the Mariel Boatlift that happened around 1980. In that time frame, Cuba was having very difficult economic times—people were hungry, the Russians weren't helping them, the problems were beyond the government's ability to cope, so they sent as many as 125,000 Cubans to the US, and among those Cubans, known as Marielitos, were many criminals, or at least people that had been in Cuban jails.

I told Diego that I did remember the boatlift. "Well," he says, "do you remember that Fidel threw in a lot of prisoners as part of the deal with Jimmy Carter?" I said, "Yeah, I remember those times... it caused a lot of controversy in the US."

Diego said, "One day I was in prison, and the next day I was in Miami." "Amazing," I said, "Why are you back in Havana?" "I was in Milwaukee for ten years, doing OK, had a good job, learned English, then... I got in a street fight, got deported—bad mistake on my part. I had to do more prison time here in Cuba, and then I got my big break—I was given a chance to sweep streets for the rest of my life... and here I am talking to you."

"I'm sorry to hear that, Diego."

"Yeah," he says, "but it was my fault... this is what I will do until I die."

So I gave him a few more CUCs. I told him I liked his Che Guevara tattoo, and he said, "Go ahead Man, take a picture."

I did, waved goodbye and said, "Buena Suerte, Diego." I continued my shopping in the marketplace—I bought a 1975 copy of Che Guevara's Diaries. I paid for the book, put it in a bag... I looked back, and Diego was gone.

Later that same afternoon, we were having lunch at an upscale restaurant overlooking the ocean, maybe three miles from the marketplace where I met Diego. I was daydreaming, looking out to sea, and I was thinking about Diego's situation, his big mistake, the Mariel Boatlift, the boat people, and from the corner of my eye, I saw him—he was pushing his trash can down the sidewalk next to the Malecón.

He couldn't see me, but I could see him. How strange that I was thinking of him, but I knew... I would never see Diego again.

San Juan

Sun all around
Pouring down
On me and the ibis —
I wave and the cabbie
In the '72 Nova gets my fare.
A fuzzy die hanging alongside Jesus
On the cracked rear view mirror —
The driver in Spanish says,

"Mira a Jesus solo colgando —
　　"Look at Jesus just hanging —
El tiene la eternidad
　　He has eternity
Para entender el objetivo de ser Dios
　　To understand the purpose of being God
Y su lugar en el cosmos
　　And his place in the cosmos.

Digo yo, "Es la verdad."
　　"So true," I say.

"A mí me gusta este coche y manejando,
　　Me, I like driving my car,
Pero, más que todo yo quiero...
　　And more than anything, I love...
Mañana."
　　Tomorrow."

Then I'm back at the hotel

The day and days hurrying by
And I realize
I don't have eternity...
To find my purpose and place.

Ted

Waterbury, CT, where I grew up, was a sports town. It was only an hour train ride to NYC. And although it was almost 3 hours to Boston, Waterburians had an affinity for Boston... because it wasn't New York. Half of the baseball fans were Yankee fans, and the other half were Red Sox fans. My family happened to be Sox fans, but I remained a steadfast Yankee fan. I was all Mickey Mantle, and my father was all Ted Williams. He was also enthralled with Jimmy Piersall, a Waterbury native who played for the Sox.

Jimmy, you may remember, was a character who was known for his antics. Because I had an aunt that knew him, I was able to meet him several times at the old Commodore Hotel in NYC. He seemed nice and all that, but I, as a ten-year-old boy, always had some trepidation that he would lash out and do something crazy. Then again, he was good friends with Dom Dimaggio who was a very normal guy.

After being with Jimmy and Dom a few times, I became more comfortable with them and I asked if they could get me to meet Ted Williams. They looked at each other and told me that Ted was... aloof, or maybe he just didn't like people coming at him. I filed the info away and never mentioned it again.

About thirty years later, I took my son to a sports dinner in Manchester, NH, because Ted Williams was going to speak. He was even more of a legend by this time in the early 80's.

After the dinner and before dessert, I took my son to the restroom and as we turned a corner, there he was—the Splendid Splinter, the greatest hitter of all time. My son tried to approach him, but that was a mistake—the legend, without making eye contact sidestepped around him and continued on his way back to the head table.

My son was disappointed that Ted wouldn't stop and talk to him. But I remembered the old days, and Jimmy and Dom telling me that it was best to leave him alone. The story may have helped to ease the rejection felt by my six-year-old son, but maybe not—he still remembers that encounter with the legend.

Six years later, I got a call from a developer who was a part owner of the Red Sox and a friend of Ted. He wanted to know if I would be interested in doing the engineering for a hunting retreat that he and Ted were planning to develop on 300 plus acres in central NH. My answer, of course, was yes. We set a date to meet and go over the ideas for the Lodge which would also include a lot of Ted's memorabilia. The general premise was to create flyways for game birds, like grouse, partridge, pheasant, quail, etc. Hunters would be located in the woods, the birds would be released along the flyways, and you can figure out what happened next.

On the day that Ted Williams was to come to the office, I instructed the staff on how they should behave.

They could not stare, they could not approach him, and they should not treat him any differently than they would any other client. The conference room had glass windows, and the employees were allowed to walk by and surreptitiously glance in at our famous guest. One walk-by per employee was all that would be allowed.

On the agreed upon day, the developer, let's call him Sam, arrived with Ted and Ted's son John Henry. Sam did the introductions, and then I escorted them to the conference room. I had been friends with Sam for years, so the initial chit-chat was comfortable and John Henry easily entered the conversation.

We moved on to the specifics about the project with John Henry doing most of the talking. His emphasis was on the lodge and the memorabilia and how the lodge would be the showcase for all the very expensive items from Ted's career that were for sale.

Ted finally joined the conversation. He wanted to talk about the flyways and the nuances of hunting game birds. He didn't seem at all interested in selling memorabilia to well-heeled sportsmen. He explained that game birds, when shot at, don't jump into the air and fly away. They continue along the flyway and follow it in a direction away from the shots. The trick is to make the flyways U-shaped with a moderately thick woods in the U. Then the birds will go around the U and the hunters, if they missed them the first time, could cut through the woods and take another shot at them—great design for the hunters, not so great for the birds.

That was as animated as Ted got that day. He then reverted to being an observer as John Henry, his young handsome son, controlled the meeting. I was impressed with JH—six feet four inches, lean and lanky, with a shock of black hair and a boatload of confidence for a twenty-something kid.

We agreed on all the general design conditions, and then set a date to meet again in two weeks. We exited to the lobby and as we lingered for a few minutes, Ted seemed to relax, so I screwed up my courage and said, "Ted, I've been wondering who you think, of all the existing baseball players playing today, might have a shot at hitting .400?"

His eyes lit up, his countenance changed—he was engaged, he was back on the ballfield. He pretended to hold a bat in his hands, as he took the typical stance of a left-handed hitter. He looked at a mythical pitcher, looked where the imagined fielders were positioned, and even glanced around at the sellout crowd overflowing the stands.

When free of his reverie, he turned to me as if to tell me the meaning of life, and he said, "Deion Sanders."

Epilogue

Sanders only played a few years of major league baseball, and without superstar success. He went on to play football in the NFL for 14 years and was inducted into the Pro Football Hall of Fame in 2011.

Interestingly, he is the only athlete to play in both a Superbowl and a World Series. He is now a sports commentator for CBS and the NFL Network. His nickname is "Primetime."

John Henry had his father cryogenically frozen upon his death in 2002. Just two years later, at the age of thirty-five, John Henry died from leukemia and, like his father, he was cryogenically frozen.

It was a beautiful September morning

... and Flight 93 left the Newark Airport heading for LA, and as a consequence, the plane was carrying a full load of jet fuel.

About twenty minutes into the flight, four members of al-Qaeda, seated in first class, left their seats and broke into the cockpit. They killed the pilots, took over the controls, and turned the plane toward the Nation's Capital.

By that time, both Twin Towers had been hit, and the North Tower would collapse within minutes of the hijacking of FL-93.

The passengers on the hijacked plane knew—they knew they were going to die. They were using cell phones to try and contact loved ones. The transcripts of their conversations show that they were remarkably stoic—they said their goodbyes and accepted their fate.

Todd Beamer was a passenger on FL-93, and he organized the resistance to the hijackers.

Meanwhile, President George Bush's Chief-of-Staff, Andy Card, was breaking the news to the President that the Country was under attack.

Back to Flight 93—some of the passengers were trying to enter the cockpit which was controlled by the terrorists. The pilot and copilot... had already been murdered.

The President, in consultation with Vice President Cheney, announced the decision to shoot FL-93 out of the sky if it did not respond, as it continued on a course towards Washington, DC. The plane was now only twenty minutes from the Capitol Building.

Inside the plane, the passengers were able to look out over the rolling fields of southwestern Pennsylvania—beautiful fields with the greens of summer slowly turning to the soft yellows and browns of Autumn. And those fields would be the last thing the passengers of the fated plane... would ever see.

Todd Beamer, along with several other passengers, finally entered the cockpit. At that point, the terrorists realized they were about to lose control, so in the name of Allah, they opted to crash the plane into the rolling fields of Shanksville, Pennsylvania.

Now there is a National Monument at the Shanksville site—an eerie monument with an all-black paved drive that marks the final flight path of FL-93. Inside the Visitor Center, there are pictures and recordings of people like George Bush and Andy Card. On large video screens, they relate some of the events that occurred on September 11th, 2001. On one of the recordings, Andy Card says to George Bush... "Mr. President, the Country is under attack." That recording will play hundreds of times a day for as long as the

Monument exists.

Only two days after returning from a trip to Pittsburg and a visit to the FL-93 Monument, I attended a party in Amherst, NH. Among the guests was... Andy Card. I walked over to him and introduced myself.

"I just returned from the Flight-93 Monument..." and he finished my sentence "... Shanksville," he said.

We talked for about ten minutes. He told me about telling the President about the attack, and how they were flying around on Air Force One trying to gather more information about the events that were unfolding.

Although most of the attack had already occurred, Flight 93 was still in the sky over Pennsylvania, and it was headed to Washington, DC. It was less than twenty minutes away.

Andy Card said that Bush and Cheney agonized over giving the order to shoot down a commercial airliner filled with US citizens as it headed towards, what they believed to be, the Capitol Building. If the plane remained on course, there would be only minutes left to execute the order.

The order was never executed, because of the actions taken by the passengers on Flight 93.

Andy Card had deep-felt emotions about the passengers and crew of Flight 93. He called the passengers on the plane true heroes who may have saved hundreds, if not thousands of American lives.

Andrew Card is a part of the history of the 9-11 attack.

Epilogue

There is some question as to whether or not it would have even been possible to scramble the fighter planes in time to shoot Flight 93 out of the sky before it reached the Capitol Building. If the plane had actually hit the Capitol, the damage to our Country would have been so much worse than it was. We all owe a debt to the heroes that were aboard that flight.

DON'T

Seventeen years—and
   Like so many   others
I remember the day.

Then the photos
Of the missing
   On walls, fences
   Church doors   anywhere
   Anyplace
   To nail your prayer —

Hope piled on hope
That the dead   might be found

The dust of flesh   blown by the wind
The screams of jumpers   echoing
                      From building to building
STILL

Lives undone
Families torn   asunder

When the pressure
   Builds   and it will —
To forget

DON'T

birds

where are the birds
when the world turns cold?
perhaps huddled
in a smoke bush, a Mugo pine,
or other shrub of mine —
i don't know.
should i shine
a light upon the shrubs   expose
their private lives, or simply...

let them be?

howl

a crescent moon waxing
two nights before May —
Leonard Cohen singing
   his final songs   smoking
   his final cigarette—and
two turkeys are perched
in a nearby tree   side by side
like lovers immersed   in life
enjoying the peace   of a mid-Spring night.

but the coyotes know,
and i know
that life is good...
if you can howl
and we do   at the moon.

the lovers have only to listen.

I'm almost sure

Wind
That draws the fire from the stove
Thumps the house with heavy blows.
Wind
Tearing shingles
Strewing snow across the road.
Wind
Finding cracks
I'm almost sure that once...
I had filled.

Dark

The moon and moonlight
On an icy night
   Slides   through the canopy
Of the so dark pines
And all the time
   I know
There   in the shadows
Just out of sight   just beyond night
What tomorrows may come
Are gathered there
Waiting
   And waiting to be.

Beware

"There is snow in the air.
   Beware   Beware!"

    I'm going out to it
    With barely a care,
    Or fear
    Of soft white death.

My days are   and have been   good.
I should never count one,
Or one million more...
As being just enough.

.

The Hill Cumorah*

It's been almost fifty years since that night in July, and I still think of it now and then. We were with two other couples, one of whom owned a hundred acre, gentleman's farm atop a drumlin, somewhere north and east of the Hill Cumorah and above the Finger Lake Region in Western New York State. Their 1920's style, upstate New York farmhouse sat on the highest part of the hill with 360-degree views of the fields and rolling hills.

As the sun set, the summer breeze cooled the fields that had baked all day beneath a cloudless sky, and the emerging darkness calmed the ever-present house flies. So at this most pleasant time of day, the floor to ceiling windows were opened wide and the air that had touched the grasses filled the house, and it felt like we had landed on one of the nicest places on Earth.

Our well-off farmer friends were in the process of restoring the farmhouse for use as a weekend retreat, where they could enjoy a bucolic lifestyle far removed from the pressures of New York City. They were doing everything right—the windows had the old style glass, the furniture was an assemblage of antiques, the beams were exposed, the floors were newly finished hard Northern pine, and supper would be served on an authentic wood-plank farmer's table.

We took our seats at the table and enjoyed an

exquisite, candle-lit meal served with the finest of New York State wines, and the finest of breezes that July had to offer found their way to the farmhouse atop the hill. The conversation was relaxed and less cerebral than had we been dining in a Manhattan high rise.

After dinner, we migrated with our drink in hand to the porch that took up the full width of the house. I picked out a rocking chair, lit up a cigar and watched the owners curl up on their romantic porch swing. The gibbous moon was still behind the trees and shrouded by low hanging clouds in the east. But there was enough of a moon to cast a soft light over the fields, and you could sense the pleasure of the flora as they enjoyed the respite provided by the cool evening air.

Judith, our hostess, declared, "The night and the moon are beckoning. Shall we take an easy walk across the fields, and experience the stars before the moon steals them from the sky?" "Well," I said, "since you described the walk so eloquently, let us all stroll along the grass-lined paths in the softness of moonlight, enjoy each other's company, and see some stars that haven't been seen in New York City since street lights were invented."

We set our glasses, cigars and cigarettes down, and followed Judith into the fields. She led us on a path that ran north and west along the ridge of the drumlin. We stopped occasionally to "feel" the stars, watch Draco wending its way between Ursa Major and Ursa Minor, and—here, beneath the most stars the six of us had seen in years—we felt... less important... than we did in the City.

As we continued our walk, I turned to the east and saw the moon climbing, pushing back the darkness of the sky over upstate New York, and yes, obliterating the stars... relentless as it moved above the trees. One by one, the stars yielded to the dominant moon. And then, looking slightly west of south, I saw a very bright light, much brighter than say, Venus, or Sirius, the brightest star in the sky. "Hey guys," I said, "look over here." They turned and stared quizzically at the light (maybe beacon would be a better word). "What is that?" we said, in harmony. I said, "I can tell you definitively, it is not Venus, or Sirius, or some star or planet."

We were speechless as we watched the light and, seemingly, as the light watched us. For a few minutes it was stationary, then it moved directly at us—we were mesmerized and didn't move as it approached. There was no noise as it continued toward us. After a minute or two of movement, it stopped directly above us. We looked up, unable to ascertain the height of the beacon... "What's going on?"

After remaining stationary, directly above us, for perhaps another minute or two—it went straight up, without a sound, and within seconds it was a pinpoint of light and... disappeared. Silence! We looked at each other, said nothing more, turned and walked to the house.

We sat on the porch... what was there to say? As highly educated people, not one of us wanted to be the first to speculate. But among the thoughts I kept to myself was, "Is it just a coincidence that we are near... The Hill Cumorah?"

*It was at the Hill Cumorah, near Manchester, NY, that the Angel Moroni revealed the golden tablets to Joseph Smith. Moroni allegedly visits Cumorah... every now and then.

.

really

```
1 x 9 + 2 = 11
12 x 9 + 3 = 111
123 x 9 + 4 = 1111
1234 x 9 + 5 = 11111
12345 x 9 + 6 = 111111
123456 x 9 + 7 = 1111111
1234567 x 9 + 8 = 11111111
12345678 x 9 + 9 = 111111111
123456789 x 9 + 10 = 1111111111
```

silly isn't it?
meaningful?   maybe
not just the numbers
but also
   the shape
   of the numbers
   when written,
also, form a pattern
like the way a stone
cast upon a pond   radiates
concentric circles —

our numbers build a trapezoid!

tell me —
does it matter   should we care,
do the patterns once seen,

   affirm that we are?

Old

Your old Dad is older
   Than you'll ever be —
And when you pull out
   Grey hairs
   Rub heat on your knees
   Squint at the print
   Fall asleep on the couch
It's then you will know —
   How the old man   must feel.

My Dad on his 86th

looking down
i look him in the eye
... "Dad,
Dad are you still there?"
  "Oh yes, I'm fine."

  a response so practiced... he's
like a Mynah   bird in a cage,

or a circling hawk on Christmas Day...
it's just another   day to fly.

  he doesn't know
  what day it is   or if

it's time to die.

Papa, must I die?

"Yes, though it will not be
For a long long time."

"But why, Papa?"

"Even now you see,
Life does not persist.
We squash the house found ants,
Branches fall from the long dead Elm,
The pansies have gone to seed.
Remember the deer, glassy-eyed
Tied to the roof of the hunter's truck?"

"I don't want to die!"

"Nor I   Nor I."
Yet   it is the way.
There isn't space in our small world
     To accumulate forever.
Had others not died,
There would be no room for you —
And without your smile,
     Your laugh, your love,
Would I want to live forever?

Without thinking twice
I would choose this time   with you."

I am the canvas

Livin' large
In a Frank Lloyd Wright
Spendin' the night
In an all-glass house
In the PA woods —

I can see out
And the deer
Can see in.

I wonder   do they ponder
The oddities of the caged
Creatures within?

But as I see it,
I'm living in a work of art.

I am the canvas for the Mona Lisa,
I am the paint   drying on the Pollock.

So you don't like Christmas?

Well, he has been quite ill of late and then you tell him that you don't like Christmas—debilitating news especially in his current condition. So he asked me, The Traveler, to write to you about Christmas.

Do you think it is a coincidence that Christmas comes near the winter solstice? It's not. Christmas was planned as a replacement for "Saturnalia," which was a time of rampant revelry, sprinkled with socially acceptable orgies. Christmas was intended to be more of a family affair with religious overtones that would, over time, replace Saturnalia.

Christmas did push aside the pagan festival, and it became a true family-oriented time of year. Of course, as the years went by, materialism began to dominate the spirit of the season and Christmas became a consumer-driven holiday. I suspect that it is the rise of materialism that has eroded your formerly warm feelings about this time of the year.

But you can resist—you can pick and choose the parts of Christmas that you let into your life. How about Handel's "The Messiah," or "Silent Night" by Mannheim Steamroller, or "Rockin' Around the Christmas Tree" by Brenda Lee? Is there any way to sit with family and friends, and listen to those songs, while the snow is snowing and the fireplace crackles, and not feel a sense of warmth and contentment?

Isn't a Christmas tree really something special? I wish I could have one all year long—just a little tree with white lights and passers-by would see the tree in the window and have thoughts like... "Gee, isn't that pretty," and maybe they would stop for a minute and think... "Well, I feel a little calmer, but I don't know why."

And what's wrong with a few small presents? Christmas is the first childhood dream. There is mystery, anticipation, good times—seeing relatives who arrive but once a year.

Speaking for myself, I put off being a jerk... from the time the tree goes up, until after the tree comes down.

Merry Christmas! And to all... have a good night.

The Traveler

Con te Partirò [I'll go with you]*

Montreal in February
  Is raw, and they may
  Or may not
Plow the snow
From empty streets   and
The sidewalks now
Are wet with snow, so
I slog through shoe-high slush
And find a music store
On a second floor
Wanting for shoppers.

And in the store
I'm astounded surrounded
By sounds
Sounds I've never heard before

    And two weeks later
    I'm falling
      falling
       maybe
       forever.

I ask the clerk
About the music—she says,
"Romanza by Bocelli and Brightman."
I must have it —
I buy two CD's

And two weeks later
  I'm falling
      falling
Through darkness accelerating
I hear   "Con te Partirò"

I want the clerk
To play it again as I walk
The aisles of a new and wondrous
World —
Lost in the songs
Lost in the sounds
Of Bocelli and Brightman.

  And two weeks later
  I'm falling
    f
      all
        ing —

  If there is a bottom
    Of the abyss,
    And if   the darkness lets me live,
    ... Con te Partirò.

*The poem attempts to conflate two events, the first being the discovery of "Romanza" by Bocelli and Brightman, and the second being the experience of stepping into an elevator only to find out that the elevator wasn't there.

the girls are gone

no girly voices   calling for "Papi,"

or looking for his finger   so
they might coax him on an explore —
they've learned   of course
he never says, "No."
an easy mark   no need
to cajole or whine
just an easy smile and

"Come Papi"   and he is on his feet

and moving.

we have been given

when first our love
was new and fresh
   we made love
   almost nightly,
and we would
   half in jest divine
the number of
nights of love
   we had yet to explore
and our guesses...

were in the thousands.

we knew, of course,
whether from infirmity, or
   certain death —
there would be
a night of love   that would be our last —

but the end to come
did not come today —
so this night
we may embrace,
make love once again,
and cherish
the day and night
we have been given.

Ever too Perfect

Is the rainbow there
    For the flowers to see?
Why is grass
    Grass?
Or trees   trees?

    All of everything
    Seems to me
Ever too perfect —

Than there is a need
    To be.

3.14159265359

Those are the first twelve numbers of the Pi sequence. It represents the ratio of the circumference of a circle to its diameter. The ratio has been calculated to 5 trillion digits, and the sequence never reaches a point of repetition. Clearly, it is an irrational number, and it seems to show up in many important mathematical calculations. Therefore, it should be celebrated... and it is. Pi day is celebrated on March 14th (i.e. 3/14) each year.

However some years, from a Pi perspective, are more important than others. For example, on 3-14-15 at 9:26:53 in the morning, we were able to celebrate a point in time that coincided with the first 10 digits of the Pi ratio. Wow! What a day that was! But those who were alive in 1592 were even more privileged. On Pi day in 1592, people experienced 3-14-1592 at 6:53:59 in the morning, which meant that they were alive at a point in time that numerically corresponded to the first 12 digits of Pi! Some people have all the luck.

On Pi day, it is customary for people throughout the world to compose a Pi poem which has a 3:1:4 sequence, such as:

Oh my my
I
Marvel at Pi

adieu

the air about   is all astir
breezes appear
jostling
leaves   and shaking branches —
clouds preen for the finale
as Ra   life-giving Ra
(please,   don't go)
bids   His bittersweet

adieu.

Acknowledgements

The author has learned that producing a second book is also a substantial undertaking, and Acknowledgements are required.

Thanks to Tom Asacker and Shannon McCarthy-Minuti for helping make this book as professional as my first book, "Time is all we have."

Many thanks to my wife for her several drawings included in this book. The drawings add depth and meaning to some of the stories and poems.

Leslie Dews once again provided insights regarding the minutia of publishing that I tend to not understand. She also provided comments on the draft manuscript.

I would like to thank the Nashua Writer's Group for their comments and creative criticism.

And lastly, I would like to thank Carol Jenisch for her continuing encouragement to pursue my writing.

About the Author

Robert Cruess was born in Mississippi, raised in Connecticut, worked in Venezuela and has lived in New Hampshire with his wife and family for over forty years.

"On only nights" is his second book with a collection of short stories and poems. His first book, "Time is all we have," was published in October, 2017.

He is a civil engineer, an award-winning developer, a writer, and, above all, a husband, father, and grandfather in love... with the life that he has.

Contact the author at rcruesspoet@gmail.com.

Made in the USA
Middletown, DE
22 December 2018